So you want to be a Leader

The top 19 +1 ways to see if you have it takes to be a great leader.

US Presidents Edition

Free evaluation tool to identify what kind of leader you are

Authored by:

Eric Erickson

SO YOU WANT TO BE A LEADER

Have you ever imagined of running a huge multi-billion dollar company? Have you ever thought about what it would be like to be the leader of a huge organization or a not for profit cause? Ever dreamt about being the President of the United States?

I think we all have aspirations to want to be the best we can. For many of us it's just trying to pay the bills each day. But, I have found that whatever you do in your life it you need to have some type of leadership ability. If you're a parent, you still need to lead you kids. You need to teach them about right and wrong. If you are just a single person trying to take care of yourself you still need to take on responsibility for yourself.

I think we all have some type of leadership abilities within us, we just need a tool to help us evaluate what those qualities are that make up a good leader.

I have researched the Internet and many books to put this together. While researching for this book I thought it prudent to write a book using quotations from past US presidents.

Why you ask?

I have always seen US presidents as the formal icon of leadership. Leadership is not just about making decisions, delegating and rising to the occasion. A leader is always prepared even for the worst moments. They have to make decisions that are for the greater good and are not always the popular decision. Most importantly, they sacrifice their time and all their energy for the greater good.

I know many of our presidents we've had in the past have not always been but you call "great leaders" but we have had many US Presidents that stepped up and have done great good in our nation. In my research efforts, I have found many US Presidents that are not common to us gave some remarkable speeches and have some great quotes.

Now my question to you is why don't we remember some of these US presidents? Is it because they were not involved in any war time efforts or times of disaster? Maybe, but all the same, the people still elected them to be their leader because they saw something in these men that was great.

As I started to write this book many asked me what makes me qualified to write this book. Where did I learn to become a leader? My earliest recollection of becoming a leader was when I was about 12yrs of age. I was in Boy Scouts at the time was asked to become a patrol leader. A patrol leader is a youth that runs the troop (group of boys) with the help of an adult leader. At the time I cannot tell you that I knew what a leader really was. But I can tell you that the adult leader, Marshall was his name, taught me how to run meetings, how to coordinate, lead the other boys in the Pledge of Allegiance, the Scout oath and Law and a lot of other things that I don't know that I took seriously. Being a leader seemed pretty simple back then. Of course I don't know how much leading I really did. At this same time in my life my parents were always pretty hard on me. They were pretty strict about making sure I got my homework and chores done and I always seemed to have to do a ton of yard work for me to do. My Dad, JC, in particular seemed to always be hard on me. He made sure that I did things right and I took responsibility for my actions. I later appreciated it because he taught me how to work hard. He always wanted to push me a little farther. I remember some days I would just cry because I could not understand why I was being pushed so hard. Little did I understand that this is where I gained most of my leadership qualities.

I must also let you know that I was a big dreamer. I always had high aspirations for myself. I was that boy that wanted to be the CEO of a large corporation. I would dream of myself sitting at a huge desk and making decisions that affected the whole world.

As I look back and wonder why that was, I can only figure that we didn't have a lot of money back then and I had to find a way out. I needed to figure out how I could be like "the rest." I obviously thought we were the only poor people. As I grew older, into my late teens, I was given many responsibilities at work to lead. I found out very quickly that becoming a leader just does not happen overnight. I think it's fair to say most of us never think about becoming a leader or ever imagined that they would be a leader. I think much of becoming a leader has to do with outstanding work ethic and sacrifice. Many of you that are leaders in your own spheres can probably agree that you had to make many mistakes to become a better leader. If you're a parent you can probably appreciate this comment. At the same time, you probably had to start at the bottom and work really hard.

I want to share a great quote from President John Adams that says,

"If you actions inspire others to dream more, learn more, and become more, you are a leader."

As you have probably noticed in your life, your actions truly dictate who you are as a person and as a leader. As you read this book remember this quote. I think it will have a different meaning to you when finish the book.

Before we get started I wanted to reiterate the purpose of this book. I hope to give you the top 20 qualities that every leader should have in order to become what I would call a great leader. I am going to utilize quotes from US Presidents as a way to portray these qualities. I also hope to add some of my experiences to push the point across. It is my objective that you will take the info from this book and use it to evaluate yourself and identify key aspects to become a better leader. I even put together a game at the end where you can evaluate yourself to identify how good of a leader you are.

In matters of style swim with the current, in matters of principle stand like a rock. Thomas Jefferson

Table of Contents

#1 - Manage change… Don't fight it

"It is not strange . . . to mistake change for progress." Millard Fillmore

After President John Taylor died suddenly on July 9, 1850, Fillmore became the 13th President of the United States. The change in leadership also signaled an abrupt political shift. Fillmore had very different views on the slavery issue. Before Taylor's death, Fillmore told him that, as President of the Senate, he would give his tie-breaking vote to the Compromise of 1850. The Compromise of 1850 was a package of five bills passed in the United States in September 1850, which defused a four-year confrontation between the slave states of the South and the free states of the North regarding the status of territories acquired during the Mexican-American War (1846–1848).

When Fillmore took office, the entire cabinet offered their resignations. Fillmore accepted them all and appointed men who, except for Treasury Secretary Thomas Corwin, favored the Compromise of 1850. When the compromise finally came before both Houses of Congress, it was very watered down. As a result, Fillmore urged Congress to pass the original bill. This move only provoked an enormous battle where "forces for and against slavery fought over every word of the bill." To Fillmore's disappointment the bitter battle over the bill crushed public support and President Fillmore announced his support of the Compromise of 1850.

Can you imagine what took place back then? John Taylor is president, suddenly dies and when Millard Fillmore becomes president nearly the entire cabinet resigns because President Fillmore felt compelled to support the Compromise of 1850. How would you feel if you were just elected President only to have no support from your advisors? It's interesting to note that President Fillmore accepted the resignation of his advisors; he did not try convincing them to stay. That is a scary situation to be in.

President Fillmore's quote is very true even today. Managing change is not easy. First we need to recognize it for ourselves. Change is inevitable, but the right change sometimes takes being committed to the change. President Fillmore was committed to the Compromise of 1850. If you go learn about the compromise it was a pivotal movement that changed the fabric of our nation.

Change in our lives is inevitable. The way you choose to manage it will change the fabric of yourself. Here are a few ways to help you to manage change:

1. Logically understand the change. Take all emotion out and just look at the change from the outside.

2. Make a list of all the pros and cons that make up the change. Remember no emotional lists.
3. Look at all the positive things that make up the change and identify how you can capitalize on it.
4. Don't look back or have regrets…. Move forward.

In conclusion, many people you come across may not believe in your change or concepts to move forward. If you are committed to the change, don't fight it. You will find those that will join with you once they see how committed you are to the cause.

#2 - Don't procrastinate

"In a moment of decision, the best thing you can do is the right thing to do. The worst thing you can do is nothing." – Theodore Roosevelt

In 1901, President McKinley was assassinated and Roosevelt became the 26th President of the United States. He attempted to move the Republican Party (GOP) toward Progressivism, including trust busting and increased regulation of businesses. Roosevelt became the first person elected to a term in his own right in 1904 after having ascended to the Presidency (from the Vice-Presidency) upon the death of his predecessor, winning the largest percentage of the popular vote since the uncontested election of 1820. Roosevelt coined the phrase "Square Deal" to describe his domestic agenda, emphasizing that the average citizen would get a fair share under his policies. As an outdoorsman and naturalist, he promoted the conservation movement. On the world stage, Roosevelt's policies were characterized by his slogan, "Speak softly and carry a big stick". Roosevelt was the force behind the completion of the Panama Canal; sent the Great White Fleet on a world tour to demonstrate American power; and negotiated an end to the Russo-Japanese War, for which he won the Nobel Peace Prize.

I thought it would be a good idea to define what procrastination is. Procrastination is the practice of carrying out less urgent tasks in preference to more urgent ones, or doing more pleasurable things in place of less pleasurable ones, and thus putting off impending tasks to a later time.

President Theodore Roosevelt is probably one of my favorite presidents for the fact that he was not afraid to make a decision. If you look at his life he had to make some significant decisions. I don't know for sure, but I would assume that he always "took the bull by the horns" and didn't shrug his responsibility as President of the United States. I am also going to assume that he learned the importance of not procrastinating from his parents. He did come from a wealthy family. You didn't become wealthy in those days if you procrastinated. The late 1800's and early 1900's were times of vision and building. Imagine what it took to get the Panama Canal built. Imagine the impact the Panama Canal has today on transportation. Billions of dollars of goods run through the Panama Canal each year. The canal helped our nation to flourish. Can you imagine what would have happened if Roosevelt procrastinated the building of that canal? It's entirely possible that the canal would have never been built.

Our lives are the same way. We think and dream of ideas and concepts each day only not to take action on them. A

12

good leader is one that takes those concepts, thinks about them and then takes action on the ones that can make a difference.

In conclusion, remember the words of President Roosevelt, "the worst thing you can do is nothing."

#3 - Be Prepared

"To be prepared for war is one of the most effectual means of preserving peace." George Washington

George Washington was elected as the first President as the unanimous choice of the electors in 1788, and he served two terms in office. He oversaw the creation of a strong, well-financed national government that maintained neutrality in the wars raging in Europe, suppressed rebellion, and won acceptance among Americans of all types. His leadership style established many forms and rituals of government that have been used since, such as using a cabinet system and delivering an inaugural address. Washington was hailed as "father of his country" even during his lifetime.

I want to note a few things about President Washington. Even though his war time efforts were extraordinary and he made substantial sacrifices for the country we live in, it is important to note the foundation that he set up (i.e. the cabinet system). This foundation laid the ground work for many successful presidents. I mention this because preparation requires a lot of work before we see the benefits. It is preparation that allows us to be qualified to make decisions. It is preparation that gives us knowledge. It is preparation that defines us and gives us direction in how we want to live our lives. If you look into Washington's life you will be amazed at all the concepts and work he put into creating this great nation. Now, I am not saying that Washington was a perfect person, but the vision he had to create these systems was brilliant.

You may ask why I chose this quote. I like this quote because it is a measurement of what can be done when you prepare. I don't think Washington loved pursuing war. I don't think he sought after war either. This was a time that sacrifices had to be made for the welfare of those that wanted religious freedom. From his quote it shows me he was always prepared for war but would rather select the peaceful route if able.

I want you to think about what preparations you make to avoid what may be the inevitable. What do you do routinely to help yourself prepare for life's challenges? Every leader should have a routine that helps them to prepare for the difficult choices. I think every leader needs to prepare for even the easy choices that need to be made. Would there be easy choices to make if we were not prepared?

#4 - Avoid busy work... delegate

"Surround yourself with the best people you can find, **delegate** authority, and don't interfere". Ronald Reagan

As the 40th president of the United States, Reagan implemented sweeping new political and economic initiatives. His supply-side economic policies, dubbed "Reaganomics", advocated reducing tax rates to spur economic growth, controlling the money supply to reduce inflation, deregulation of the economy, and reducing government spending. In his first term he survived an assassination attempt, took a hard line against labor unions, announced a new War on Drugs, and ordered an invasion of Grenada. He was re-elected in a landslide in 1984, proclaiming that it was "Morning in America". His second term was primarily marked by foreign matters, such as the ending of the Cold War, the 1986 bombing of Libya, and the revelation of the Iran–Contra affair. Publicly describing the Soviet Union as an "evil empire", he supported anti-communist movements worldwide and spent his first term forgoing the strategy of détente by ordering a massive military buildup in an arms race with the USSR. Reagan negotiated with Soviet General Secretary Mikhail Gorbachev, culminating in the INF Treaty and the decrease of both countries' nuclear arsenals.

Delegating seems to be one of the most difficult qualities to achieve. Delegation is defined as the passing down of authority and responsibility to another person to carry out specific activities. Most leaders do not have a hard time passing work or activities on to others. The difficulty lies in that the leader does not understand they are still responsible for the outcome of the delegated task. Most great leaders when delegating will find the right person for the job, then they will explain in great detail the expectations of the task and then ask the person to return and report. Great leaders know just because they have "pawned" a task off to another, they are still responsible for the outcome of the task. Take the example of Ronald Reagan, look at all he accomplished in his time as president. It is obvious that he had to delegate many of the responsibilities to achieve what he did. But here is the key, almost all the items he delegated were done in such a way that the person that was given the responsibility of the task completed the task just as President Reagan would have it carried out. In other words, it was almost like President Reagan was there.

Great leaders just don't delegate responsibilities just so they have more time to golf. Great leaders delegate responsibility to teach those they lead how to lead. Leaders are tasked to empower their people and do so by delegating tasks. I learned a long time ago that leaders are always training their replacements. Why is that so? I will leave that one for you to decide.

#5 - Continue to grow

"You ain't learnin' nothin' when you're talkin'." Lyndon Johnson

Lyndon Johnson, 36th President of the United States, succeeded to the presidency following the assassination of John F. Kennedy on November 22, 1963. He completed Kennedy's term and was elected President in his own right, winning by a large margin in the 1964 election.

Before Johnson entered into politics he was a teacher. He talks Mexican-American children and then went on to teach public speaking at a high school.

Johnson had a lifelong commitment to the belief that education was the cure for both ignorance and poverty, and was an essential component of the American Dream, especially for minorities who endured poor facilities and tight-fisted budgets from local taxes. He made education a top priority of the Great Society, with an emphasis on helping poor children. After the 1964 landslide brought in many new liberal Congressmen, he had the votes for the Elementary and Secondary Education Act (ESEA) of 1965. For the first time, large amounts of federal money went to public schools. In practice ESEA meant helping all public school districts, with more money going to districts that had large proportions

19

of students from poor families (which included all the big cities).

I find it humorous that Johnson seemed to be a well educated man, yet the semantics of his quote are a little off. Here you have a president that really changed the education system of the US. It shows how important education is. When I talk about continuous learning it is important to know that formal schooling is not the only place we can learn. Reading books, going to seminars and other self-educating things can be done. I find myself on the road a lot so I enjoy audio books.

If you look at the majority of our US Presidents you will find a great deal of education under their belt. You find that many of them were educated at great universities. Many of them went to school for many years to get the education they needed to pursue their futures.

Here are some tips that I would suggest to help you master this topic. Set aside time each day to forward your learning. Pick topics that make you feel inadequate. Studying these subjects will help you to gain more self esteem, build your vocabulary and polish your skills that you have mastered. Lastly, always continue to listen.

#6 - Feedback

"Nearly all men stand adversity, but if you want to test a man's character, give him power." — *Abraham Lincoln*

Abraham Lincoln was the 16th President of the United States, serving from March 1861 until his assassination in April 1865. Lincoln led the United States through its greatest constitutional, military, and moral crisis—the American Civil War—preserving the Union, abolishing slavery, strengthening the national government and modernizing the economy. Reared in a poor family on the western frontier, Lincoln was self-educated, and became a country lawyer.

I think Lincoln was called honest Abe for a reason. He always held true to his beliefs and stuck to them like glue. Lincoln was really had a tough life. He lost children when they were young; he lost his first wife to fever and many other hard ships. He always seemed to persevere. He taught himself law, and got the emancipation proclamation passed. Lincoln empowered many. He was liked by many and obviously disliked by those with slaves.

This is really an interesting quote. I had a hard time finding a quote to fit this topic. I chose this quote from Lincoln because feedback is meant to help someone improve or to empower them to do better. I am amazed at what society teaches, that feedback is meant to be critical and negative. We would rather down trodden a person than lift them up. A great leader can see the good in people. A great leader can re-kindle the fire within someone and help them to be better. When I think of ways that I have been taught to give feedback they have always been kind and respectful.

Here are some tips that I would suggest to use when giving feedback. These tips will help empower those you influence.

1. Use a moderate tone of voice
2. Be genuine and concerned
3. Show an interest in what they are doing
4. Give positive feedback to the things they are doing right
5. Be direct and straight forward in correcting the individual
6. Do not rely on not factual stories, simply state the facts

If you remember my statement before that you are always training your replacement. You may find the individuals that you spend the most time giving positive feedback are the ones are training as your replacement.

#7 - Honesty

"I pray Heaven to bestow the best of blessing on this house (the White House) and on all that shall hereafter inhabit it. May none but honest and wise men ever rule under this roof!" John Adams

Too bad this quote has not held true.

John Adams was the second president of the United States. He was a leading advocate of American independence from Great Britain. Adam played a leading role in persuading Congress to declare independence. He assisted Thomas Jefferson in drafting the Declaration of Independence in 1776.

Before the presidency Adams felt acutely that he had a responsibility to live up to his family heritage: he was a direct descendent of the founding generation of Puritans, who came to the American wilderness in the 1630s, established colonial presence in America, and had a profound effect on the culture, laws, and traditions of their region. Journalist Richard Brookhiser, drawing on the relevant historiography, has written that these Puritan ancestors of Adams's "believed they lived in the Bible.

My first thought I had when I read a bit of Adams biography was about honesty. Is honesty learned when we are young or is it something that we need to learn as we get older? I remember as a kid when I got in trouble for being dishonest, I really got in trouble. It was almost that my parents were embarrassed that I even thought about doing such a thing. I know that in my life it took several situations for me to recognize honesty from dishonesty. In fact, in my family honesty was learned at a young age.

Can you recollect your childhood and remember if you were taught honesty at a young age? I have no scientific proof but, I think it is harder to learn honesty when you're older or especially if your parents and siblings were not honest.

What does it take to be honest? Is honesty always the best policy? Do we not even think about the importance of honesty in our lives?

I think there are a few ways to answer these questions. Many people believe in a supreme being or a God. For those people, I included, it is a desire to want to do better because God would not be dishonest with us. It is through that example that makes us want to follow. For those of other faiths or no faith at all, sometimes it is a moral or an ethical code of conduct in which they follow.

SO YOU WANT TO BE A LEADER

Regardless of what you believe, it is important to know in order to become a good leader you need to be honest at all costs.

#8 - Have a Good Conscience

"Above all, tell the truth."Stephen Grover Cleveland

Cleveland was the 22nd and 24th President of the United States. Cleveland is the only president to serve two non-consecutive terms. Cleveland took strong positions and was heavily criticized. Even so, his reputation for honesty and good character survived the troubles of his second term.

President Cleveland had to make several difficult choices as president. He was even accused of many things that were not necessarily his fault. But he learned one important thing in life which was to always tell the truth. This did not always prove to be the popular choice. Many times he was greatly ridiculed and the newspapers would make up the most horrendous cartoons about him.

That being said, there is a reason for using this quote. The decisions you make as a leader will not always be the popular decision. It may not even be the right decision according to the world. There is one thing that always will hold true in the end, you told the truth. There is a popular phrase that people say when it comes to having a good conscience. It is something to the effect that "at least I will sleep well tonight."

You may agree, but I have had several times in my life where telling the truth was probably the worst thing I could do. I still did it. The ramifications were not the most desirable. But I did sleep well knowing that I was forth right.

I would dare say that having a good conscience is probably one of the most desired qualities that leaders want in their lives. I don't know that every good leader is perfect, but I think every good leader aspires to telling the truth even though the situation may not call for it. President Cleveland shares a story when he found out that he had something cancerous in his mouth. He did not want anyone to know so he secretly had surgery to get the cancer out of this mouth and told the public something different. Now, is that cause to be alarmed? Probably not, but telling the truth may or may not have hurt him.

That leads me to another reason for telling the truth. We are very good at what I call the "little white lie." I know I have had my fair share of those. What I have noticed in my life is once you get good at the little white lie what stops you from telling the big white lie and then the lie that ends up putting you in jail. I think having a good conscience is not always the easiest thing to do, but that is why this is such an important characteristic of being a great leader.

#9 - Never look Backward

"I walk slowly, but I never walk backward." Lincoln

Abraham Lincoln was the 16th President of the United States, serving from March 1861 until his assassination in April 1865. Lincoln led the United States through its greatest constitutional, military, and moral crisis—the American Civil War—preserving the Union, abolishing slavery, strengthening the national government and modernizing the economy.

This is really a pretty amazing quote. Here you have a president that is still battling slavery and trying to bring a country together. Because of Lincoln our nation is not divided.

What did Lincoln mean to never look backward? I want you to think about your life and remember the times when you looked back on old memories or maybe mistakes that you made. How did you feel? What did you learn? My assumption is that Lincoln has taught us that there is nothing wrong with moving slowly forward, but don't look back at the things that kept you back. We as individuals work so hard at trying to move forward, whether it is in our careers or our personal lives. Many times we experience our weaknesses and our short comings. So, what do we do to move forward?

Do we need to create action? Do we need to get ourselves off the floor and dust the dirt off our pants and move forward?

A good leader is a good leader for many reasons, one of the most important reasons they are a good leader is they understand how to look the good, the bad and the ugly in the face and continue to move forward. It is amazing to me how many people I see that suffer from job loss or hard times only to quit. A good leader cannot afford to quit. It is not in their nature. A good leader has worked too hard to just stop. Do some good leaders take a little longer than others to get up and move forward? Of course, that is human nature. But a good leader will not stand still for long. Even if they know they might fall again, a good leader is willing to take that chance.

#10 - Dare to Dream

"We grow great by dreams. All big men are dreamers. They see things in the soft haze of a spring day or in the red fire of a long winter's evening. Some of us let these dreams die, but others nourish and protect them; nurse them through bad days till they bring them to the sunshine and light which comes always to those who sincerely hope that their dreams will come true." Thomas Woodrow Wilson

Thomas Woodrow Wilson was the 28th President of the United States. Wilson was over ten years of age before he learned to read. His difficulty reading may have indicated dyslexia. But as a teenager he taught himself shorthand to compensate.[1] He was able to achieve academically through determination and self-discipline. Wilson worked very hard and eventually became an intellectual with very high writing standards. He even went on to become a leader of the Progressive Movement and even served as President of Princeton University.

It would be tough to say that Wilson was one of our better Presidents. Many thought of him as racist. The point that I want to make with this is here is a man that had severe problems reading and goes on to becoming the president of one of the most prestigious universities in the US and also becomes President of the US. How does someone do that? I would suppose that you need to have some pretty big dreams.

Its dreams that help us to become what we want to be. It is dreams that help to something bigger than us. It is through dreams that we are who we are today.

Do you like to dream? What type of things do you dream about? Do you dream of changing the world? Do you dream of world peace? Do you dream of having that beautiful house down by the beach?

A great leader always has great dreams. Whether they are dreams to change the world they live in or just to change what may seem like an insignificant part of their life.

I would encourage you to take a minute to just close your eyes for a few minutes, clear your head and just dream a little.

#11 - Believe you can

"If you don't feel something strongly you're not going to achieve." George Walker Bush

George Walker Bush was an American politician and businessman who served as the 43rd President of the United States of America. Bush graduated from Yale, was a good business man and also co-owned the Texas Rangers baseball team. Bush had to deal with probably the biggest terrorist threat to our nation. He also dealt with Hurricane Katrina that obliterated many Gulf States. Bush was a popular president to many, but also had many enemies due to some of his decisions.

There is much to say about Bush. Here is a man that for the most part has seen success in his life. He obviously worked very hard to achieve the great results he had.

I want you to think for a minute about a time that you achieved success. It does not need to be a huge success. It can be something as small as getting a great grade on a college paper, or even successfully asking a man or woman on a date. What did it start with? What did you envision? Did the plan you envisioned work? What was the end result?

I am of the opinion that you cannot achieve something if you don't have some type of vision or belief to know what the end needs to be. Or you want it to be. Many people go through life on an average or standard routine. They are satisfied with their job, they are always putting themselves down, they always hang out with people that put themselves down and really do not want anything more. A great leader is never satisfied, never gives up and always wants to challenge life to see what life gives back.

In order to attain this understanding that you cannot achieve or succeed in life without a self-belief or some self-esteem that you are capable of achieving anything you put your mind to. I want to tell you some of the concepts that I do in order to believe in myself and achieve what I put my mind to.

1. Envision the goal you want to complete. It needs to be very detailed.

2. Start preparing yourself for the thing you want by going over in your mind the details of the event.

3. Create a detailed plan and envision yourself actually completing the event. This is very important because your mind is very powerful; it will help you to come up little details that you may not have thought about.

4. Practice in your mind what you are going to say to those you need to communicate with and practice what you will say to various objections you may incur.

#12 - Cooperation

It's amazing what you can accomplish if you do not care who gets the credit. Harry S Truman

Harry S. Truman was the 33rd President of the United States. The final running mate of President Franklin D. Roosevelt in 1944, Truman succeeded to the presidency on April 12, 1945, when Roosevelt died after months of declining health.

When Truman took over the presidency it was a very difficult time. Germany had surrendered and the war with Japan was assumed to continue. Truman asked Roosevelt's cabinet to stick with him and support him and they did. Truman had to make one of the biggest decisions of his term by dropping the atomic bomb on Japan. It was not really understood how terrible the casualties would be, but in order to preserve dangers put upon the USA he made the decision.

When great leaders make big decisions it is important to recognize that they do not make these decisions without counseling their team or trusted advisors. A great leader for obvious reasons takes full accountability and responsibility for decisions, but they typically do not take all the credit when the outcome is overwhelmingly successful. As Truman stated, great leaders want to make it happen. They rarely care about taking the credit.

How does a great leader get to the point where they are not selfish but self-less?

How does a great leader get to the point where they are willing to delegate success?

How does a great leader get a team to cooperate for the great good?

These are very typical questions that great leaders ask themselves when they want to create success.

How well do you cooperate with others? Are you willing to delegate success to others without regret?

My invitation to you is to identify your goals and ask yourself are they selfish or self-less. All great leaders are willing to deny themselves the crown for the good of the team. I learned long ago that you should always council with your councilors, those that you that trust and rely on.

I believe that you have to work very hard to cooperate with others. Cooperating with others means that we need to let down our guard and be willing to share our ideas and be prepared to receive comments that can be viewed as criticism. Do you have what it takes to accept criticism for the success of the project?

A great leader can only learn cooperation when they are willing to cooperate with others.

#13- Be Decisive

"Assess the risk of each option as well as the benefits," he says. "These practices will increase confidence that you've selected the alternative that is the best balance of risk and reward." Lincoln

Can you imagine the risk of trying to abolish slavery? People were dying! The white people that wanted to protect the black people got killed. Here you have a President of the US trying to get rid of segregation and change the nation. How many times do you think he got death threats? A lot. But here is the difference between a regular person and a leader? They are decisive, they know what they want and NO ONE will change their mind because they are confident in their decision.

I need to confess. I have had a hard time with this my whole life. I don't know if it's my Dyslexia. I don't know if my little mind cannot wrap my head around it. But here is the difference. I work really hard to fight and hold onto my dream as hard as I can. There is not a day that does not go by that I am not focused on what I decided to do 20yrs ago. I decided that I would be self-employed. I decided to be a leader. I decided to make a difference for myself and for others. There is not a day that goes by that I don't remember what I decided to do.

A great leader needs to make that ONE big decision. A great leader needs to decide what they are going to do to make that difference, that one thing that is going to change the way you are going to be and what you are going to believe in.

You need to decide right now what you are going to decide what to do and why you are doing it. You need to be like President Lincoln. You need to decide what you believe in and go with it. Will there be risks? Yes. Will it be hard? Yes, but the difference between you being a great leader and just another leader is that you need to decide what you are going to do

What will you accomplish by doing this? You will achieve greatness. I believe that everyone is destined for greatness. You just need to find it, believe in it and be decisive and stick to it.

#14 - Courage

"Honest conviction is my courage; the Constitution is my guide." Andrew Johnson

I want to use the Wikipedia definition of courage. Courage is the ability and willingness to confront fear, pain, danger, uncertainty, or intimidation. Physical courage is courage in the face of physical pain, hardship, death, or threat of death, while moral courage is the ability to act rightly in the face of popular opposition, shame, scandal, or discouragement.

When I was researching this specific topic I never put much thought to the difference between physical and moral courage. I think that I have always combined the two together.

Great leaders are always faced with decisions that directly affect their courage. Great leaders are seen and known as great leaders because they stand out from the crowd. They stand tall because they know without a shadow of doubt that they can hold their head high and be confident that they have made good judgment calls.

The fact is that every great leader will be challenged by others. They will challenge their integrity, honesty and even their morals. It is up to the great leader to always make sure they are making good, even righteous decisions.

We all know what is right and wrong. It is what we do with our right and wrong decisions that identifies how courageous we are.

Many will do anything it takes to shred you of every bit of integrity and moral values you have, but it will depend on how courageous you are to fight and stand up for what you believe in.

My invitation to you is that you look back on your life and identify how you have lived your life, how you have made decisions and how others perceive you.

This will help you identify if you need to change you way of thinking or if you need to stay focused on your righteous and moral behaviors.

#15 - Do it Right

"It is easier to do a job right than to explain why you didn't."
Martin Van Buren

We don't do a task just to say we did it. It is something that we need to learn from. There were many times when I was a kid when my Dad used to drag me to a service project. Whether it was working at the church welfare farm or picking weeds for some old lady. Did I always do the job that was asked of me, sure I did. Did I do it right? I am not sure that I can say that I did. Do you remember when you were a kid and your mom asked you to do something and you did it and went back to what you were doing. Then she told you to get back and do the job right. That happened to me a lot when I was a kid.

Why do we let ourselves do a job that is really not done correctly? The answer that I have come up with is we have no desire to do that job in the first place so why should I waste my time doing it. I see this all the time with employees. They really need the job but they do want to be doing what they are tasked to do to get the money. So what happens, they do it really slow or they just don't do it at all because someone else will come by and do it for them.

I also see managers and leaders do this same thing. They are tasked to complete this job and because they don't want to do it they give it to one of their employees to do and they do a below average job because they don't have the knowledge to complete the task.

A great leader sometimes has to "suck it up" and realize that being a great leader requires you to do things that you may not want to do. I want to share with you a secret. Over my 25+ yrs of experience in managing and leading I have found that doing the things that may be lower than me or I maybe to good for has taught that the value to work. It has taught me that if I am going to be the best I can be I need to learn how to do every task right. I have found great pride in myself when I accomplished a task to the best of my ability. I have found that I am a better person when I take the time to learn the task and just do the best I can.

Here are some tips to help you to do it right.

1. Take a deep breath and tell yourself that this is a good learning experience
2. Take it seriously and tell yourself that you are going to do your best
3. As you go through the task create points where you can get excited and appreciate your success

#16 - Develop Good Relationships

"We have nothing in our history or position to invite aggression; we have everything to beckon us to the cultivation of relations of peace and amity with all nations."
Franklin Pierce

Franklin Pierce was the 14th President of the United States. He made many friends, but he suffered tragedy in his personal life; all of his children died young. As president, he made many divisive decisions which were widely criticized and earned him a reputation as one of the worst presidents in U.S. history.

Philip B. Kunhardt and Peter W. Kunhardt reflected the views of many historians when they wrote in *The American President* that Pierce was "a good man who didn't understand his own shortcomings. He was genuinely religious, he loved his wife, and he reshaped himself so that he could adapt to her ways and show her true affection. He was one of the most popular men in New Hampshire, polite and thoughtful, easy, and good at the political game, charming and fine and handsome. However, he has been criticized as timid and unable to cope with a changing America.

Here is a President that probably has the worst reputation as a US President in the history of the US and yet I am going to use a quote from him. This time period the US was separated mainly because of slavery. There was a lot of unrest and the people were really uneasy. So you can imagine how difficult it was to develop good relationships. What was interesting to me is even though he was the president of the United States at a time of separation he still had a relationship with the confederate president Jefferson Davis, which of course all the North states appalled. Now, I cannot tell you the reason why President Pierce had a relationship with the confederate president, but he was known as an overall nice guy.

One relationship I would like to pay attention to is the one between Pierce and his wife. I find it's the relationships that we want are the ones that we work really hard to build. Even though Pierce was very well liked in his state of New Hampshire he was a very unpopular president.

Do you go the extra mile to develop relationships you want? What steps do you take to make sure you develop long lasting relationships?

Here are some things to consider when building relationships.

1. Build relationships with those that have common interests and beliefs. This does not mean they have to go to the same church as you, but certainly you want them to have the same basic beliefs.

2. Understand that building relationships requires work from both parties. It requires both individuals to make a solid relationship.

3. Build relationships with the end in mind. You want to build lasting relationships. If you can see yourself befriending the other person for a long time, that would be a relationship worth cultivating.

4. Be willing to make sacrifices to help each other out. I loved how Pierce took so much time out of his busy life to spend time with his wife and catered to her. Friendships are about supporting and helping.

#17 - Be an Example

"That's all a man can hope for during his lifetime—to set an example—and when he is dead, to be an inspiration for history." William McKinley

William McKinley was the 25th President of the United States. He was assassinated in September 1901, six months into his second term. McKinley led the nation to victory in the Spanish–American War, raised protective tariffs to promote American industry, and maintained the nation on the gold standard in a rejection of inflationary proposals. Rapid economic growth marked McKinley's presidency. He promoted a tariff to protect manufacturers and factory workers from foreign competition. This was a man that got things done. He was well known for doing so.

When we talk about who the examples are in our lives, what qualities come to mind? I think they will be different for each of us. Think of the various examples you have had in your life. Whether they were people, things or places. When we strive to become better or to grow we tend to find good examples in our lives. Many times these examples come right when we need them because we subconsciously look for them.

Most often good leaders are not good leaders because they were able to figure it all out on their own. If you were to ask any great leader who they looked up to or who they could depend on they would most certainly tell you many stories of people they looked up to. I think that goes for most successful people. Those that have achieved great things, big or small; can tell you that they could not have done it without the help of certain people in their life.

A good leader often becomes that person who gives the great advice or helps the person seeking for growth opportunities. A good leader also is also the one that is not afraid to tell someone like it really is.

Being an example is really a difficult pursuit. We all make mistakes in our lives only to hope we don't do them again. Then most good leaders hope that they can use those experiences to touch others and build something great.

#18 - Always give your Best

"Always give your best, never get discouraged, never be petty; always remember, others may hate you. Those who hate you don't win unless you hate them. And then you destroy yourself." Richard Nixon

Nixon was the 37th president of the United States serving two terms. We know from the history books that he resigned from office in his second term. We don't need to make this a big history lesson but President Nixon did in fact have some haters in his life. Nixon had a pretty tough tour as president. Between the Vietnam War and the threats of communism he always tried to do his best.

I picked this quote for a very specific reason. As a great leader it is your duty to always do your best despite what others will think of you. The catch is as a great leader that when people hate you that you don't hate back. As President Nixon says it will destroy you. Great leaders are great because they don't let the haters bother them. As I said before, great leaders have self control and are much disciplined.

I have had many people ask me what does it mean to do your best. Is your best going to be better than the next person? Is there a measurement that determines what give your best means? For me, doing my best means that I have done everything that I know and have applied it in the very best way that I know. Now do others know more than me? Absolutely. That does not mean that we don't have the tools, knowledge and experience to do our best in the situation given to us.

Some word of caution, do not compare you to others. This will also destroy you and make you feel low and you can destroy yourself.

Always remember that everyone is destined for greatness. Our greatness is determined by looking back and telling yourself that you did the very best you could do.

#19 - Discipline

Discipline is the soul of an army, it makes small numbers.
George Washington

As the first president of the United States and serving two terms in office, I often think about George Washington. I know many people have mixed feeling about our first president and what he did for our country. One thing does ring true is that he was much disciplined. He was very regimented. He really believed in the cause. I am sure that Washington had many discouraging times, but he was a very disciplined man. I think Washington could actually envision what he wanted the end result to be.

Andrew Cayton had this to say about Washington,
"Washington had a vision of a great and powerful nation that would be built on republican lines using federal power. He sought to use the national government to preserve liberty, improve infrastructure, open the western lands, promote commerce, found a permanent capital, reduce regional tensions and promote a spirit of American nationalism."

What does discipline mean? Wikipedia says Discipline is the assertion of willpower over more base desires, and is usually understood to be synonymous with self control. Self-discipline is to some extent a substitute for motivation, when one uses reason to determine the best course of action that opposes one's desires.

What does it take to be disciplined?

- Self Control
- Motivation
- Vision
- Study
- developing a system

I am sure there are several other words to describe what it takes to be disciplined.

What does it take for a great leader to learn discipline? One of the great lessons I have learned in my up and downs of being a leader is that you need to know the vision believe in the vision and have enough self control and motivation to carry out your role as a leader.

Discipline comes from knowing what you want and doing what it takes to carry out that task. Many times discipline is the force behind motivating ourselves in spite of a negative emotion. Discipline requires hard work and persistence.

One of the ways that I have gained my discipline is knowing that I have a family to take care of financially. We all have various reasons to be disciplined.

I would suggest if you are struggling with this is to write down the things that motivate you. What is it that makes you tick each day and then create a regiment that will allow you to continue motivating yourself and help you to get past the negative emotions and trying times.

#20 - Passion

"Always bear in mind that your own resolution to succeed, is more important than any other one thing." Abraham Lincoln

Abraham Lincoln was the 16th President of the United States. As we know in history, President Lincoln's sincere desire was to free the slaves and re-unite a nation. Can you imagine how much fighting and how much pressure he went through to free the slaves and re-unite the United States of America? I don't know that Lincoln was the most popular president of our nation, but he was resolute, he had more passion to want to see slaves freed and a nation re-united that he was assassinated. Lincoln was assassinated by a man that had enough passion to think he could keep the confederate nation alive. Booth was an actor and led the appearance like he was acting out a scene when he killed Lincoln. Passion can be such a driving force that people throughout history have died for their cause. It was the passion of men that signed the Declaration of Independence. Their lives were on the line every day to make their opinion known to England. Many of them were killed in that cause.

What drives you each day? What makes you wake up in the morning and say "this is a new day, what am I going to do to make it a success?"

SO YOU WANT TO BE A LEADER

A great leader has to have the passion of Lincoln. A great leader needs to have the passion of our founding fathers. A great leader needs the passion, the vision to believe in something so much that they will go further than the average person to succeed. A great leader breaks down barriers and builds solid foundations. A great leader stands tall and expresses his/her vision to the world.

That is passion.

How does one get that passion? I love the movie City Slickers. Billy Crystal sets out of another adventure with his two buddies. This time to help move cattle from point A to point B. Despite all the problems facing Billy Crystal and his buddies, Billy gets to know Jack Palance, the head cowboy. In talking with Jack Palance, Billy Crystal finds out that there is one thing that can create clarity, solve problems and make him happier. Billy Crystal learns that one thing is different for us all. When we find it, it will make all the difference in the world.

I share this movie with you simply because to have passion it requires that ONE THING. You need to find that one thing yourself. It is different for all of us. I promise you will know when you figure it out. It will be like a bright light that pops on in your head. It will be so clear that all perspective comes into focus.

Evaluation

This is your time to honestly evaluate yourself on what type of leader you are. This is very difficult for most because most people will not be honest with themselves.

I want you to think of this as your first project to see what kind of leader you are. If you are willing to evaluate yourself honestly you are on your way to becoming a great leader.

How this works. As you go through each chapter in this book, rate yourself on a scale of 1 – 5. One being that you have a lot to learn and five being that you are exceptional in that area.

SO YOU WANT TO BE A LEADER

Once you have rated yourself, add up the total and see where you fit in the rating scale.

1. Manage change –   _____
2. Don't procrastinate –   _____
3. Be prepared –   _____
4. Avoid busy work –   _____
5. Continue to grow –   _____
6. Feedback –   _____
7. Honesty –   _____
8. Have a good conscience –   _____
9. Never look backward –   _____
10. Dare to dream –   _____
11. Believe you can –   _____
12. Cooperation –   _____
13. Be decisive –   _____
14. Have courage –   _____
15. Do it right –   _____
16. Develop good relationships –   _____
17. Be an example –   _____
18. Always give your best –   _____
19. Discipline –   _____
20. Passion –   _____

TOTAL: _____

Rating Scale:

90 – 100	You are an exceptional leader. Your desires are self-less and others surround themselves around about you because they want to with people that are successful.
80 – 89	You have great ability to become an exceptional leader. Fine tune your skills and practice them with others.
70 – 79	I would invite you to go back through this book and re-evaluate the type of person you are. Then take the specific steps to learn how you can be better. Always be positive in your journey to become a great leader and remember to let others help you in your desire to be a great leader.
60 – 69	Some are great leaders and others are great examples to great leaders. This score does not mean you are a horrible leader, it just means that you need to re-evaluate if becoming a great leader is in your future. Do not give up on your dreams to be what you aspire to be. Surround yourself with great leaders so you can identify what it takes to be a great leader.
Less than 59	It takes an exceptional person to read this entire book and then honestly rate themselves to realize that this may not be your path. Have courage that you are willing to go the extra mile and be strong in your desires to obtain what you want to achieve.